Learning to Get Along®

Listen and Learn

Cheri J. Meiners, M.Ed.
Illustrated by Meredith Johnson

free spirit
PUBLISHING®

Library of Congress Cataloging-in-Publication Data
Meiners, Cheri J., 1957–
   Listen and learn : learning to get along / Cheri J. Meiners.
      p. cm.
   ISBN 1-57542-123-2
   1. Listening—Study and teaching (Early childhood)—Activity programs. 2. Attention—Study and teaching (Early childhood)—Activity programs. 3. Social skills—Study and teaching (Early childhood)—Activity programs. I. Title.
LB1065.M373 2003
372.69044—dc21

                                                                                          2002152117

eBook ISBN: 978-1-57542-800-0

Free Spirit Publishing does not have control over or assume responsibility for author or third-party websites and their content.

Reading Level Grade 1; Interest Level Ages 4–8;
Fountas & Pinnell Guided Reading Level H

Cover and interior design by Marieka Heinlen
Edited by Marjorie Lisovskis

20 19 18 17 16 15 14 13
Printed in China
R18861213

Free Spirit Publishing Inc.
Minneapolis, MN
(612) 338-2068
help4kids@freespirit.com
www.freespirit.com

Dedication

To David and our children
Kara, Erika, James, Daniel,
Julia, and Andrea,
for listening!

Acknowledgments

I wish to thank Meredith Johnson for her beautiful illustrations. I also thank Judy Galbraith and all those at Free Spirit who believed in this series. Special thanks go to Marieka Heinlen for the lovely design and to Margie Lisovskis who, as editor, has contributed her wonderful expertise and creativity. Finally, I am grateful to Mary Jane Weiss, Ph.D., whose insight, skill, and caring have done much to advance the field of teaching social skills.

There is so much to learn about the world.

Listening helps me learn.

At school, I listen when my teacher talks.
I want to hear and understand.

When I listen,
I use my body, my eyes, and my ears.

I stay quiet. When my mouth and body are quiet, everyone can hear.

I look at the person who is speaking.
I watch what the speaker does.

Watching helps me understand
the speaker's ideas.

I think about what I hear.

Thinking helps me learn and remember.

Sometimes I listen carefully,
but I don't understand.

I can ask questions.

Sometimes I am in a group.
In the group, I can tell my ideas.

I can answer questions, too.

My teacher and classmates listen when I talk.

I like being part of the group.

Sometimes my teacher gives directions.

I look and listen carefully.

I want to hear and understand
so I know what to do.

When I listen and do what I'm asked to do,
I'll be ready for what comes next.

It might be something really fun!

Sometimes it's easy to listen.

Sometimes it's hard to listen.
There may be other things to see and hear.

I can keep trying to watch
and listen to the speaker.

Each time I listen, I get better at it.

Sometimes I listen and talk
with other children.

My friends like it
when I listen to them.

I like it when they listen to me.
Everyone likes to be heard.

Listening and talking helps me
solve problems.

I can listen to how someone feels.

The person can listen to how I feel.

Listening helps us understand each other.

At home, I listen and talk with my family.

We talk about our day.

We make plans.

We solve problems.

We learn together.

We show we care
by talking and listening.

Whenever I listen, I keep my body still.
I keep my mouth and hands quiet.

I watch with my eyes
and hear with my ears.

I think about what is said.

When I listen, I know I'm growing up.
I'm showing respect. I'm learning.

And that feels great!

Ways to Reinforce the Ideas in *Listen and Learn*

As you read each page spread, ask children:

- What's happening in this picture?
- Who's listening? How can you tell that the person is listening?

Here are additional questions you might discuss:

Pages 1–3

- What are some things the people in the picture are learning about?
- Why is it important to listen when the teacher talks?

Pages 4–9

- How do you use your body when you listen?
- How do you use your eyes when you listen?
- What are some ways listening helps you learn?
- What three things do you do when you listen?
- How does keeping quiet (looking at the speaker, thinking about what you hear) help you when you listen? How does it help other people?

Pages 10–11

- What does it mean to listen *carefully?*
- How can you get help if you don't understand something?

Pages 12–13

- What are some times we listen as a group?
- Why is it important to listen quietly in the group?
- Have you ever tried to hear a story when someone was making noise? What happened?
- How do you know when it's your turn to speak?

Pages 14–17

- Why is it important to listen to directions?
- What might happen if you don't hear the directions?
- How can we be sure everyone hears them?

Pages 18–19

- What are some times when it's easy to listen? Why is it easy to listen then?

Pages 20–21

- What are some times when it's hard to listen? Why is it hard?

- What can you do if you need help listening? *(In talking about distractions and listening, you may find it helpful to explain and discuss concepts like paying attention, ignoring other sounds, listening with "my whole self," or even "tuning in" and "tuning out" as ways to stay focused on listening. The language you choose will depend on the children. Some children may also find it easier to listen when holding something or sitting close to the teacher.)*

Pages 22–23

- How does it feel when someone listens to you?

- How do you think other people feel when you listen to them?

- Why is it nice to be listened to?

Pages 24–25

- What are some times when listening and talking can solve problems?

- What happens if people don't listen to each other when there's a problem?

- Have you ever tried to solve a problem when someone wasn't listening? What happened? Did you solve the problem? How would listening have helped?

Pages 26–27

- What are some things you like to talk about with your family?

- How does listening help people in families get along?

Pages 30–31

- Who are these children listening to? Why are they listening?

- What do you do with your body (mouth, hands) when you listen?

- How do your eyes help you listen?

- What is respect? How does listening show respect? *(You might explain respect by saying, "When you show respect to people, you show that you think they are important. Listening shows that you think a person's ideas are important.")*

Listening Games

Preparation: Photocopy the page that follows onto card stock; laminate the page if possible. Cut out the cards and place them in an envelope.

Note: The cards depict situations from preschool through grade 2. If some of the scenes won't be familiar to your group, adapt them to fit. You will also want to adapt the games' procedures if you are playing with an individual child rather than a group.

Who's Listening?

Level 1

Set out the two larger cards labeled "Careful Listening" and "Can Listen Better." Draw a card from the envelope, or have a child draw the card. Read or have a child read the card aloud. Ask: "Is this careful listening?" If it is, invite children to explain why. Then place the card in the "Careful Listening" pile. If it isn't, place the card in the "Can Listen Better" pile.

Level 2

After playing Level 1, collect the cards from the "Can Listen Better" pile. One at a time, read or have children read the cards and ask, "How can this child listen better?" or "How can this child be a more careful listener?" Reinforce the three listening skills (keep quiet, look at the speaker, think about what you hear) as well as responses about using the body, eyes, and ears and showing respect.

Listening Role Plays

Level 1

In this level, you enact scenes with the children. Draw a card from the envelope. Read it to a child or children who will then help you act out the scene on the card. Ask children, "What's happening? Is this careful listening?" If it isn't, ask children, "What would be a better way to listen?" or "What would be a more careful way to listen?" Have children help you act out the group's suggestions.

Level 2

In this level, children enact the scenes with less help from you. Have a child draw a card from the envelope. Read it to a child or children who will then act out the scene on the card. Ask children, "What's happening? Is this careful listening?" If it isn't, ask, "How can the person listen better?" or "What would be a more careful way to listen?" Have children act out the suggestions.

Level 3

Talk about other listening situations. Write children's suggestions on blank slips of paper or blank cards you have made, read them aloud, and invite children to enact them. Add the new cards to your set of listening situations and use them in future games.

Careful Listening		Can Listen Better	
Cara folded her work-sheet into an airplane because she already knew what the teacher was saying.	The teacher told children to put their names on their papers. Luís was the first one done.	At recess, Luís's friend was explaining a new game, but Luís got bored and decided to leave.	When the teacher explained something new, Luís looked at her and thought about what she said.
Luís whispered to his neighbor while the teacher told the group how to line up for the field trip.	While the teacher was talking to the class, Luís was looking under the table for his pencil.	Cara didn't under-stand what the teacher was talking about, so she drew on the back of her paper.	Cara was watching another class walk by, and she didn't hear the teacher say it was time for music.
During storytime, the children sat on the floor. Cara played with her friend's hair	Cara listened to the directions for choosing a partner for a game, and found her partner right away.	When another child gave a book report, Cara was wondering what she would say for her turn.	During reading group, Cara followed along in the book as the children took turns reading.
During show-and-tell, Cara looked at her friend and heard him tell about a rock he found when he was camping.	During spelling, Luís was counting his crayons and didn't hear the spell-ing word.	During art time, Luís watched his friends goof around and didn't hear the teacher say it was time to clean up.	At lunch, Luís talked to his friend about the past weekend. The friend said she went to the movies with her family.

Free Spirit's Learning to Get Along® Series

Help children learn, understand, and practice basic social and emotional skills. Real-life situations, diversity, and concrete examples make these read-aloud books appropriate for childcare settings, schools, and the home. *Each book: 40 pp., color illust., S/C, 9" x 9", ages 4–8.*

Also by Cheri J. Meiners

The Free Spirit Being the Best Me! series helps children learn, understand, and develop attitudes and character traits that strengthen self-confidence and a sense of purpose. Each book focuses on a specific attitude or character trait, such as optimism, courage, resilience, or work ethic. Also includes an activity guide for adults. *Each book: 40 pp., color illust., 11¼" x 9¼", ages 4–8.*

www.freespirit.com
800.735.7323

Volume discounts: edsales@freespirit.com
Speakers bureau: speakers@freespirit.com